THE
VERITABLE
BLACK DRAGON
or the
INFERNAL FORCES
SUBJUGATED TO MAN

UNICURSAL

Copyright © 2024

Translation by M-A Ricard

Éditions Unicursal Publishers
unicursal.ca

ISBN 978-2-89806-619-1 (Paperback)
ISBN 978-2-89806-620-7 (Hardcover)

First English Edition, Ostara 2024

THE
BLACK
DRAGON

OR THE
INFERNAL FORCES
SUBJUGATED TO MAN

EVOCATIONS
CHARMS & COUTER-CHARMS
MARVELLOUS SECRETS
THE HAND OF GLORY
THE BLACK HEN

Do not read in this Book
in the evening, from 1 to 3 and from 7 to 9
nor at midnight.

I conjure you, Book, to be useful and profitable to all those who will read you, for success in their affairs.

I conjure you, once again, by the virtue of Jesus Christ, each day, by the chalice, to be useful to all those which will read you.

I exorcise you in the name of The Very Holy Trinity

In the name of the Very Holy Trinity

In the name of the Very Holy Trinity.

The Mark of the Spirit

Fig. 1

GREAT PENTACLE OF SALOMON

Fig. 9

Fig. 10

Fig. 11

Fig. 12

Fig. 13

Fig. 14

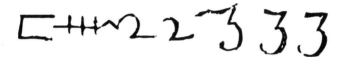

Fig. 15

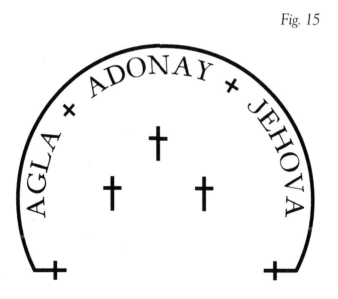

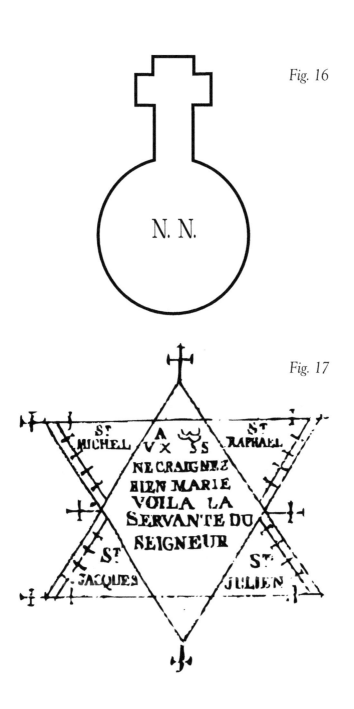

Fig. 16

N. N.

Fig. 17

St MICHEL

St RAPHAEL

A
V X S

NE CRAIGNEZ
BIEN MARIE
VOILA LA
SERVANTE DU
SEIGNEUR

St JACQUES

St JULIEN

Fig. 18

Fig. 19

✝

This book is the science of good and evil. Whoever you are, gentle reader, young or old, rich or poor, happy or unhappy, if your heart is tormented by avarice, throw this book into the fire, lest it be for you the source of all evil, the cause of your ruin and total loss. If, on the contrary, you possess Faith, Hope, and Charity, keep it as the most precious treasure of the universe. Thus, have been warned.

You are free in your actions, but do not forget that a strict account will be asked of you for the use you have made of the treasures that I put at your disposal. As for me, servant of God, I decline all responsibility, having only written this book for the good of Humanity.

✝

Prelude

F RIEND reader, allow me to take your hand and take a few steps on the arduous path that is laid out for you in this work. Listen carefully to my advice and make good use of it. This is not a trivial thing, in fact, to have direct relationships with demons, because they are our greatest enemies, to you, to me and to all humanity, and every time they can bring misfortune upon us, there is relief and joy for them.

They will show themselves to you, according to your character, that is to say, either weak, gentle, considerate, polite and affable, or noisy, hotheaded and threatening, with the aim of either deceiving you or intimidating you, always for your loss and their relief. With calm, firmness and your right, it will be easy for you to avoid their traps.

As soon as they appear in before the Circle, begin by ordering them to repress all anomalies they might have created: cold, heat, noises, bad smells, etc., and once this is achieved, make them solemnly swear not to do it again in the future.

Do not accept anything from them hand to hand, and let all material things that you require be thrown without damage in the part of the Circle you will have indicated to them. Never lose sight of the fact that this said Circle is your safeguard; inside, you are the master and king, outside, you would be at the subdued to the evil Spirit.

Sometimes, while performing a project of philosophical operation, you may notice something abnormal in the air you breathe or under your roof you, but do not worry; it is the Spirit agitated in its impotence at preventing the realization of your projects; he knows your most secret thoughts, but he can do nothing against you.

The Circles or pentacles are made with blessed chalk or blessed charcoal. By blessed chalk we must understand that it is chalk which will have remained on or under the altar cloth during the mass or, if we cannot better, simply on the blessed stone; and by blessed coal, coal taken from the boxwood of the blessed cross. For the latter, you will do the following. Go to the cemetery and take some boxwood from the cross which you will take back home to keep with care, because it will be useful to you on more than one occasion. One morning, while a mass is being said in the church of your parish, light a small fire in your house with dry, new wood, that is, parts of wood that have not been taken from a piece having previously served some profane use, then put in the pieces of boxwood intended to be changed into charcoal. To collect the burnt boxwood, you can use tongs made of new wood, and any new box will act as a damper.

Before beginning any philosophical operation, take care to purify your hands and your body.

Make your Circle following all the rules of the art, with a diameter of at least twelve feet and so that there is no free space, because this would be a door for the evil Spirit.

Always take with you, in the Circle, holy water and a blessed branch, so that the demon cannot do you any harm; but to be sure of being obeyed in everything without fraud or deception, equip yourself with the Mysterious Fork, which is obtained in the following way.

Firstly, buy without haggling, a knife whose blade is of pure steel. And on the day that suits you best, go into the woods before sunrise. The moment this star appears on the horizon, cut a branch of wild hazel, having about three feet, to serve as a handle, then go to a locksmith who will make you a small straight fork with two teeth from the blade of your knife. Do not trust anyone in this matter, and let everything be done by you or before you. Speak and command the unclean being while holding this book in your left hand and the Fork in your right hand; this in a horizontal position, the iron turned towards the Spirit. A table can be the repository of all the aforesaid objects, but they must always be within reach. If you wish, keep a paschal candle lit for the entire duration of the operation, or burn brandy Spirits in a lamp intended solely for this purpose. As a result, in case of disobedience of the Spirit, your strength will be increased by putting the teeth of the Fork in the flame, but never make inappropriate use of this means.

Several people can stand together in the Circle, but only one, the *Karcist*, must speak to the Spirit; the others must remain silent, even if the demon questions or threatens them.

The present discourse complements everything that is said further on the same subject, so be careful to interpret my thoughts correctly. Know that everything that is written in this book must be followed to the letter, while drawing benefit from my advice depending on the circumstances. Thus, the demon will always require a pledge from you, and you cannot refuse him; you must not even let him go without giving him a pledge. Never agree to give him an object taken from your body, hair, blood, etc.; you must understand that you cannot throw him your handkerchief either, since a handkerchief that you use will contain substances taken from your body. The same goes for certain other items that he might ask of you. Apart from the pledges stipulated in the following conjurations, what you must do is put your hand in your pocket and throw him a penny or the first coin you will find. When not specified otherwise, the pledge must be made immediately before reading the license to depart. For philosophical work which requires a large number of sessions, find a way, but only accept any convention incapable of causing you any harm, either presently or in the future: you have the means to make yourself obeyed, do it.

If the demon were to disappear without your consent, that is to say without you having read the license to depart, put your Mysterious Fork into the flame, or otherwise reread the conjuration and, as soon as he reappears, reproach him strongly his disobedience, then continue your work. In no case should you leave the Circle without having read the *Conjuration and the License to depart of the Spirits.* You will find prayers at the end of this book. I urge you to read some of them before setting foot outside this enclosure.

The Spirit will never come to you without being called by heart as well as by mouth, which proves to you once again that you must be firm and unshakable in your will. If you carry out the Operation of the Sign, once the Spirits are in your presence, command their leader to make himself known to you and throw to the latter a small round piece of virgin parchment, conjuring him to put his sign there, that is to say his Seal. He will then return it to you and you will stick it to the first page of your book. This operation done, that is to say the book being approved and accepted, all difficulty remains overcome, for you or those who will read you, in the future operations. You can read this book from start to finish, without danger to you, at permitted times; you must even do it often, in order to be well aware of the smallest details of any operation that you may have to carry out.

Friend reader, take advantage of the treasures that I have gathered for you in this work; be happy and pass on earth doing good. Farewell.

FIRST PART

EVOCATIONS

CONJURATION
OF THE DEMONS

In the name of the Father, and of the Son, and of the Holy Spirit: Alert, come all Spirits. By the virtue and power of your King, and by the seven crowns and chains of your Kings, all Spirits of the underworld are constrained to appear to me before this Circle, whenever I call them. Come, all of you, at my command, to do all that is in your power, being commanded. Come then from the East, the South, the West and the North. I conjure and command you, by the virtue and power of Him who is three, Eternal, equal, who is God invisible, consubstantial; and a word, which created the sky, the sea, and everything under the Heavens.

The following must be said before signing the book.

I conjure and order you, Spirits, all and as many as you are, to receive this Book in good grace, so that all the times we read the said book, or that it is read, being approved and recognized to be in form and value, you have to appear in beautiful human form when you are called, in accordance with the judgment of the reader. In all circumstances shall you harm the body, soul and Spirit of the reader, nor will you cause any pain to those in his company, whether by murmuring, by storms, noise, thunder, scandals, nor by lesions, deprivation of execution of the commandments of the said Book. I conjure you to come as soon as the conjuration is made, in order to execute, without delay, all that is written and mentioned in its proper place in the said Book. You will obey, you will serve, you will teach, you will give, you will do everything that is in your power in the usefulness of those who will order you, all without illusions. If, by chance, one of the conjured Spirits cannot come or appear when he is required, he will be bound to send others clothed with his power, who will solemnly swear to carry out everything that the reader may ask, conjuring you all by the Most Holy Names of the Almighty and Living God. Eloym, Jah, El, Eloy, Tetragrammaton, to do all that is said above. If you do not obey, I will constrain you to a thousand years of pain, or if any of you does not receive this Book with total resignation to the will of the reader.

Then, you will command the sign to be affixed and, having done so, you will throw a pledge and read the following Conjuration:

CONJURATION AND DISMISSAL OF THE SPIRITS

Show the Pentacle of Solomon and say:

B ehold your sentence which forbids you from rebelling against our wishes, and which commands you to return to your abodes. May peace be between you and us, and be ready to return whenever you are called to do my will.

CONJURATION OF THE FOUR KINGS

These four Conjurations can be said every day and at any time, and the Operator will make use of the Great Pentacle or Circle of Solomon. If we only wish to speak to one Spirit, we will name only one at the choice of the reader.

CONJURATION OF THE KING OF THE EAST

I conjure and invoke thee, O powerful King of the East MAGOA, by my holy labour, by all the names of Divinity, by the name of the All-Powerful: I command thee to obey, and to come to me, or that failing, forthwith and immediately to send unto me N., currently Masseyel, Asiel, Satiel, Arduel, Acorib, to respond concerning all that I would know and to fulfill all that I shall command. Else thou shalt come verily in thine own person to satisfy my will; which refusing, I shall compel thee by all the virtue and power of God.

CONJURATION OF THE KING OF THE SOUTH

O Egym, great King of the South, I conjure and invoke thee by the most high and holy Names of God, do thou here manifest, clothed with all thy power; come before this circle, or at least send me forthwith Fadal, Nastraché, to make answer unto me, and to execute all my wishes. If thou failest, I shall force thee by God Himself.

CONJURATION OF THE KING OF THE WEST

OBayemon, most potent King, who reignest in the Western quarter, I call and I invoke thee in the name of the Divinity. I command thee by virtue of the Most High, to send me immediately before this circle the Spirit N. Passiel, Rosus, with all other Spirits who are subject unto thee, that the same may answer in everything, even as I shall require them. If thou failest, I will torment thee with the sword of fire divine; I will multiply thy sufferings, and will burn thee.

CONJURATION OF THE KING OF THE NORTH

O thou AMAYMON, King and Emperor of the Northern parts, I call, invoke, exorcise, and conjure thee, by the virtue and power of the Creator, and by the virtue of virtues, to send me presently, and without delay, Madael, Laaval, Bamulhae, Belem, Ramat, with all other Spirits of thine obedience, in comely and human form. In whatsoever place thou now art, come hither and render that honour which thou owest to the true living God, who is thy Creator. In the name of the Father, of the Son, and of the Holy Ghost; come therefore, and be obedient, in front of this circle, without peril to my body or soul. Appear in comely human form, with no terror encompassing thee. I conjure thee, make haste, come straightway, and at once. By all the Divine names Sechiel, Barachiel; if thou dost not obey promptly, Balandier, suspensus, iracundus, Origratiumgu, Partus, Olemdemis et

Bantatis, N., I exorcise thee, do invoke, and do impose Most High commandment upon thee, by the omnipotence of the living God, and of the true God; by the virtue of the holy God, and by the power of Him who spoke and all things were made, even by His holy commandment the heaven and earth were made, with all that is in them. I adjure thee by the Father, by the Son, and by the Holy Ghost, even by the Holy Trinity, by that God whom thou canst not resist, under whose empire I will compel thee; I conjure thee by God the Father, by God the Son, by God the Holy Ghost, by the Mother of Jesus Christ, Holy Mother and perpetual Virgin, by her sacred heart, by her blessed milk, which the Son of the Father sucked, by her most holy body and soul, by all the parts and members of this Virgin, by all the sufferings, afflictions, labours, agonies which she endured during the whole course of her life, by all the sighs she uttered, by the holy tears which she shed whilst her dear Son wept before the time of His dolorous Passion and on the tree of the Cross, by all the sacred holy things which are offered and done, and also by all others, as in heaven so on earth, in honour of Our Saviour Jesus Christ, and of the Blessed Mary, His Mother, by whatsoever is celestial, by the Church Militant, in honour of the Virgin and of all the Saints. In like manner, I conjure thee by the Holy Trinity, by all other mysteries, by the sign of the Cross, by the most precious blood and water which flowed from the side of Jesus Christ, by His Annunciation, and by the sweat which issued from His whole body, when He said in the Garden of Olives: My Father, if it be possible, that these things pass from me, that I may not drink from the chalice of death; I conjure thee by His death and passion, by His burial and glorious resurrection, by His ascension, by the coming of the Holy Ghost. I adjure thee, furthermore, by the crown of thorns which was set upon His head, by the blood which flowed from His feet and hands, by the nails with which He was nailed to the tree of the Cross, by the five holy tears which He shed, by all which He suffered willingly through great love of us: by the lungs, the heart, the hair, the inward parts, and by all the members, of Our Saviour Jesus Christ. I conjure thee by the judgment of the living and the dead, by the Gospel words of Our Saviour Jesus Christ, by His preachings, by His sayings, by all His miracles, by the child in swaddling clothes, by the crying child, borne by the mother in her most pure and virginal womb; by the glorious intercession of the Virgin Mother of Our Saviour Jesus Christ; by all which is of God and of His Most Holy Mother, as in heaven so on earth. I conjure thee by the holy Angels and Archangels, and by all the blessed orders of Spirits, by the holy Patriarchs and Prophets, by all the holy Martyrs and Confessors, by all the holy Virgins and innocent Widows, and by all the saints of God, both men and women. I conjure thee by the head of St. John the Baptist, by the milk of St. Catherine, and by all the Saints.

CONJURATION

Very Powerful Conjuration for all days and hours of the Day or Night, being for Treasures hidden by men or Spirits, that the same may be possessed and transported.

I command you, O all ye Demons dwelling in these parts, or in what part of the world soever ye may be, by whatsoever power may have been given you by God and our holy Angels over this place, and by the powerful Principality of the infernal abysses, as also by all your brethren, both general and special Demons, whether dwelling in the East, West, South, or North, or in any side of the earth, and, in like manner, by the power of God the Father, by the wisdom of God the Son, by the virtue of the Holy Ghost, and by the authority I derive from Our Saviour Jesus Christ, the only Son of the Almighty and the Creator, who made us and all creatures from nothing, who also ordains that you do hereby abdicate all

power to guard, habit, and abide in this
place; by whom further I constrain and
command you, *nolens volens,* without guile
or deception, to declare me your names,
and to leave me in peaceable possession
and rule over this place, of whatsoever
legion you be and of whatsoever part of
the world; by order of the Most Holy
Trinity, and by the merits of the Most
Holy and Blessed Virgin, as also of all
the saints, I unbind you all, Spirits who
abide in this place, and I drive you to the
deepest infernal abysses. Thus: Go, all
Spirits accursed, who are condemned to
the flame eternal which is prepared for
you and your companions, if ye be rebellious and disobedient. I conjure you
by the same authority, I exhort and call
you, I constrain and command you, by
all the powers of your superior Demons,
to come, obey, and reply positively to
what I direct you in the name of Jesus
Christ. Whence, if you or they do not
obey promptly and without tarrying, I
will shortly increase your torments for

a thousand years in hell. I constrain you therefore to appear here in comely human shape, by the Most High Names of God, Hain Lon, Hilay, Sabaoth, Helim, Radiaha, Ledieha, Adonay, Jehova, Ya, Tetragrammaton, Saday, Massias, Agios, Ischyros, Emmanuel, Agla, Jesus who is Alpha & Omega, the beginning and the end, that you be justly established in the fire, having no power to reside, habit, or abide in this place henceforth; and I require your doom by the virtue of the said names, to wit, that St. Michael Angel drive you to the uttermost of the infernal abyss, in the name of the Father, and of the Son, and of the Holy Ghost. So be it.

I conjure thee, Acham, or whomsoever thou mayst be, by the Most Holy Names of God, by Malhame, Jac, May, Mabron, Jacob, Desmedias, Eloy, Aterestin, Janastardy, Finis, Agios, Ischyros, Otheos, Athanatos, Agla, Jehova, Homosion, Aja, Messier, Sother, Christus vincit, Christus regnat, Christus imperat, Increatur Spiritus sanctus.

I conjure thee, Cassiel, or whomsoever thou mayest be, by all the said names, with power and with exorcism. I warn thee by the other sacred names of the most great Creator, which are or shall hereafter be communicated to thee; hearken forthwith and immediately to my words, and observe them inviolably, as sentences of the last dreadful day of judgment, which thou must obey inviolately, nor think to repulse me because I am a sinner, for therein shalt thou repulse the commands of the Most High God. Knowest thou not that thou art bereft of thy powers before thy Creator and ours? Think therefore what thou refusest, and pledge therefore thine obedience, swearing by the said last dreadful day of judgment, and by Him who hath created all things by His word, whom all creatures obey. *P. per sedem Baldarcy et per gratiam et diligentem tuam habuisti ab eo hanc nalatima namilam,* as I command thee.

CONJURATIONS

For each day of the week.

Monday
Conjuration to Lucifer

I conjure thee, Lucifer, by the living God, by the true God, by the holy God, who spoke and all was made, who commanded and all things were created and made. I conjure thee by the ineffable name of God, On, Alpha & Omega, Eloy, Eloym, Ya, Saday, Lux les Mugiens, Rex, Salus, Adonay, Emmanuel, Messias; and I adjure, conjure, and exorcise thee by the names which are declared under the letters V, 6, X, as also by the names Jehova, Sol, Agla, Rissasoris, Oriston, Orphitue, Phaton ipreto, Ogia, Speraton, Imagnon, Amul, Penaton, Soter, Tetragrammaton,

Eloy, Premoton, Sirmon, Perigaron, Irataton, Plegaton, On, Perchiram, Tiros, Rubiphaton, Simulaton, Perpi, Klarimum, Tremendum, Meray, and by the most high ineffable names of God, Gali, Enga, El, Habdanum, Ingodum, Obu Englabis, do thou make haste to come, or send me N., having a comely and human form in no wise repulsive, that he may answer in real truth whatsoever I shall ask him, being also powerless to hurt me, or any person whomsoever, either in body or soul.

This experiment is performed between eleven and twelve, and between three and four. It will take coal, and consecrated chalk to compose the circle, about which these words must be written: *I forbid thee, Lucifer, in the name of the Most Holy Trinity, to enter within this circle.* The pledge that suits him is a live mouse. The master must have a stole and holy water, an alb also and a surplice. He must recite the Conjuration in a lively manner, commanding sharply and shortly, as a lord should address his servant, with all kinds of menaces: Satan, Rantam, Pallantre, Lutais, Cricacœur, Scircigreur, I require thee to give me very humbly... &c.

Tuesday
Conjuration to Frimost

I conjure and command thee, Frimost, by all the names wherewith thou canst be constrained and bound. I exorcise thee, Nambrosth, by thy name, by the virtue of all Spirits, by all characters, by the Jewish, Greek, and Chaldean conjurations, by the confusion and malediction, and I will re-double thy pains and torments from day to day for ever, if thou come not now to accomplish my will and submit to all that I shall command, being powerless to harm me neither in body or soul, nor those in my company.

This experiment is performed at night, from nine until ten. We must give him the first stone found during the day. It is to be received with dignity and honour. We Proceed as on Monday: compose the circle, and write about it: *Obey me, Frimost, obey me, Frimost, obey me, Frimost.*

Wednesday
Conjuration to Astaroth

I conjure thee, Astaroth, wicked Spirit, by the words and virtue of God and of Jesus Christ of Nazareth, unto whom all Demons are submitted, who was conceived of the Virgin Mary; by the mystery of the Angel Gabriel, I conjure thee; and again in the name of the Father, and of the Son, and of the Holy Ghost; in the name of the glorious Virgin Mary, and of the Most Holy Trinity, in whose honour do all the Archangels, Thrones, Dominations,

Powers, Patriarchs, Prophets, Apostles, and Evangelists sing without end; Holy, Holy, Holy, Lord God of Hosts, who art, who wast, who art to come, as a river of burning fire. Neglect not my commands, refuse not to come. I command thee by Him who shall appear with flames to judge the living and the dead, unto whom is all honour, praise, and glory. Come, therefore, promptly, obey my will, appear and give praise to the true God, unto the living God, yea, unto all His works; fail not to obey me, and give honour to the Holy Ghost, in whose name I command thee.

This experiment is performed at night, from ten to eleven; it is to obtain the good graces of the King and others. Write in the circle as follows: *Come, Astaroth, come, Astaroth, come, Astaroth.*

Thursday
Conjuration to Acham

I conjure thee, Silcharde, by the image and likeness of Jesus Christ our Saviour, whose death and passion redeemed the entire human race, who also wills that, by His providence, thou appear forthwith in this place. I command thee by all the Kingdoms of God. Act; I adjure and constrain thee by his Holy Name, by Him who walked upon the asp, who crushed the lion and the dragon. Do thou obey me, and fulfill my commands, being powerless to do harm unto me, or any person whomsoever, either in body or soul.

This experiment is made at night, from three to four, at which hour he is called, and appears in the form of a King. A little bread must be given him when he is required to depart; he renders man happy and also discovers treasures. Write about the circle as follows : *By the Holy God, by the Holy God, by the Holy God.*

Friday
Conjuration to Bechard

I conjure thee, Bechard, and constrain thee, in like manner, by the Most Holy Names of God, Eloy, Adonay, Eloy, Agla, Samalabactany, which are written in Hebrew, Greek and Latin; by all the sacraments, by all the names written in this book; and by him who drove thee from the height of Heaven. I conjure and command thee by the virtue of the Most Holy Eucharist, which hath redeemed men from their sins; I conjure thee to come without any delay, to do and perform all my biddings, without any prejudice to my body or soul, without harming my book, or doing injury to those that are in my company.

This experiment is performed at night, from eleven to twelve, and a nut must be given to him. Write within the circle: *Come Bechard, come Bechard, come Bechard.*

Saturday
Conjuration to Guland.

I conjure thee, O Guland, in the name of Satan, in the name of Beelzebuth, in the name of Astaroth, and in the name of all other Spirits, to make haste and appear before me. Come, then in the name of Satan and in the names of all other Demons. Come to me, I command thee, in the name of the Most Holy Trinity. Come without inflicting any harm upon me, without injury to my body or soul, without maltreating my books, or anything which I use. I command thee to appear without delay, or, that failing, to send me forthwith another Spirit having the same power as thou hast, who shall accomplish my commands and be submitted to my will, wanting which, he whom thou shalt send me, if indeed thou comest not thyself, shall in no wise depart, nor until he hath in all things fulfilled my desire.

This experiment is performed at night, from eleven to twelve, and as soon as he appears burnt bread must be given him, and ask him anything you will, and he will obey you immediately. Write in his circle: *Enter not, Guland, enter not, Guland, enter not, Guland.*

Sunday
Conjuration to Surgat

I conjure thee, Surgat, by all the names which are written in this book, to present thyself here before me, promptly and without delay, being ready to obey me in all things, or, failing this, to dispatch me a Spirit who will bring me a stone which shall make me invisible to everyone, when-soever I carry it. And I conjure thee to be submitted in thine own person, or in the person of him or of those whom thou shalt send me, to do and accomplish my will, and all that I shall command, without harm to me or to any one, so soon as I make known my intent.

This experiment is performed at night, from eleven to one. He will ask for a hair on your head; but you have to give him one of any animal, and force him to ac-cept it. This is to discover and transport all treasures, and anything that you may will. Write in his circle: *Tetragrammaton, 3. Ismael, Adonay, Ilma.* And in a second cir-cle: *Come Surgat, come Surgat, come Surgat.*

Fig. 2

Circle and Characters of Lucifer

Fig. 3

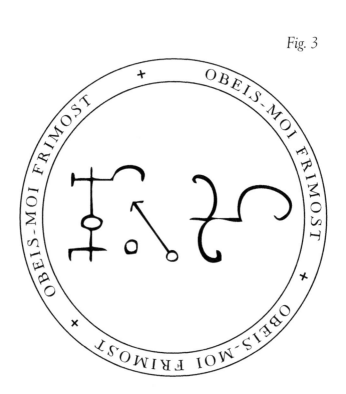

Circle and Characters of Frimost

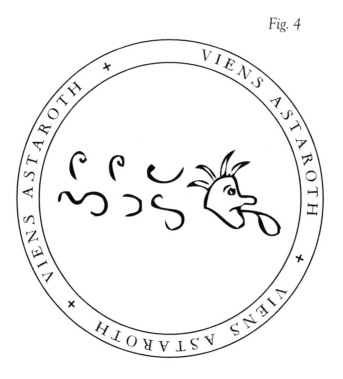

Fig. 4

Circle and Characters of Astaroth

Fig. 5

Circle and Characters of Silcharde

Fig. 6

Circle and Characters of Bechard

Fig. 7

Circle and Characters of Guland

Fig. 8

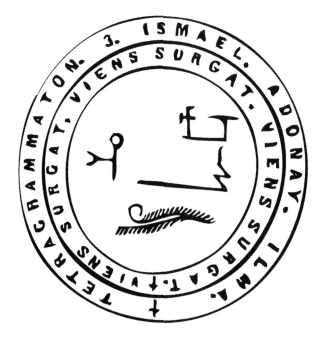

Circle and Characters of Surgat

SECOND PART

CHARMS &
COUNTER-CHARMS

To lift all Spells, and bring in the person who caused the harm.

Take the heart of a completely dead animal, taking care not to injure it in any way; and put it on a clean plate, then have nine hawthorn needles, and proceed as follows.

Pierce the heart with one of your needles, saying: "Adibaga, Sabaoth, Adonay, *contra ratout prisons pererunt fini unixio paracle gossum.*"

Take two of your needles and pierce, saying: "*Qui fussum mediator agros gaviol valax.*"

Take two more, and while piercing, say: "*Landa zazar valoi sator salu xio paracle gossum.*"

Take again two of your needles, and while piercing, say: "*Mortus cum fice sunt et per flagellationem Domini nostri Jesu-Christi.*"

Finally, pierce using the last two needles with the following words: "*Avir sunt* (before you) *paracletur strator verbonum offisum fidando.*" Then continue, saying:

"I call upon those, men or women, who have had the Missal of Abel made; coward, it was done wrong that leaving to come find us by sea or by land, from everywhere, without delay and without disdain."

Pierce then the heart with a nail to these last words. Note that if you cannot get hawthorn needles, you will use new nails.

Once the heart has been pierced, as described above, place it in a small bag and hang it from the chimney, high enough so it cannot be seen. The next day, take the heart out of the bag, put it on a plate, removing the first needle you will pierce it anew in another place of the heart, saying the intended words above. You will remove two more; and piercing them again, will say the appropriate words. Finally, you will remove them all in the same order to

pierce them again as before, observing
never to pierce in the same hole twice.
Continue this experiment for nine days.
However, if you don't want to give any
rest to the evildoer, do your novena on
the same day, and in the order prescribed.

After having finally pierced the heart
with the nail, uttering the intended words
for this purpose, build a large fire; put the
heart on a grill, to roast it on the glowing
embers. The evildoer must come to beg
for mercy. Otherwise if it is out of his
power to come within the short time you
grant him, you will cause him to die.

Note well that you must prevent,
either by blocking the door, or by any
other means, the evildoer from approaching your grill.

To lift and destroy all curses celebrated against animals.

Take a cup of salt, more or less, depending on the quantity of cursed

animals; pronounce on it the following: *"Herego gomet hunc gueridans sesserant deliberant amei."*

Make three circles around the animals, starting at the side of the rising sun, and continuing following the course of this star, the animals in front of you, and making your jets on them by pinch, reciting the same words.

The Sympathetic Mirror.

This mirror, which has the shape indicated in Figure 9, is double-sided, flat on one side and magnifying on the other. These two sides are respectively called the small and the large side of the mirror. The sympathetic mirror is used in some counter-charm operations to discover the evildoer. We look at ourselves, sometimes from one side and sometimes from the other, while pronouncing the words indicated, and, at a given moment, the face of the operator disappears and is replaced by that of the evildoer who comes and goes more or less often.

When working to deliver a person whose illness is already very advanced, we are sometimes obliged to touch the sick person with the mirror while repeating the mysterious words said in the counter-charm operation.

Moreover, the sympathetic mirror has certain natural virtues, including those of curing dull and rheumatic pain in general. To do this, we touch the part of the body in pain, sometimes with one side of the mirror and sometimes with the other, without looking at which side we start, each time dedicating the patient to three saints, saying for example: "*Saint Joseph, Saint John, Saint James, I beg you to heal* N."

Repeat three times, and then say three *Pater* and three *Ave* while making the sign of the cross before and after. Instruct the patient to rub the pain with fingers moistened with saliva, once a day for three days, and then say, each time, three *Pater* and three *Ave*, as above.

To obtain such a mirror, we buy a two-sided mirror in conformity with the sympathetic mirror, and, in an evocation, we conjure a Spirit to recognize "*the virtues stipulated in the Book*", which he cannot refuse. In the event that he asks to touch the mirror, it should be thrown to him and ordered to put it back in the circle "*without cracks and endowed with the aforementioned virtues.*"

This mirror must not be put to any profane use.

Of the Talisman,

Its Construction, its Virtues.

On the eve of Midsummer between one and two in the morning, go where there is wild Periwinkle or small Periwinkle. You can grow them in your garden, or in flowerpots, as long as in the latter case, the pots are placed so that you have to leave your home to go near them. You will pick the plant silently and take it into your house, taking care not to look behind you, even if you hear footsteps behind your heels; no harm may befall the operator during this journey, all the animals fleeing at his approach. It will be kept for the following purposes.

As much as possible, pick the first branch that comes before your eyes when you open the box containing the picking above. Remove the head and put it in a small piece of white paper, then complete the number of leaves, adding what is necessary, from the same branch to have nine; then add camphor as big as a pea and fold. As soon as the paper is folded in half, and therefore you will no longer see its contents, continue to fold the paper, saying:

1° If you want to use the packet as a talisman: "For N. (name the person) dwelling at... whom we want to preserve from all evils for N... once *vassis atatlos vesul & cremus, verbo san hergo diboliâ herbonos,* twice *vassis atatlos, &c.,* thrice *vassis, &c.*" Repeat the prayer three times.

2° If you want to use it to break and destroy an evil spell: "For N. dwelling at... whom we want to cure from an evil spell, if any, and against such and such, once *vassis atatlos vesul & cremus, verbo san hergo diboliâ herbonos;* twice *vassis atatlos, &c.,* thrice *vassis, &c.*" Repeat three times.

While making the packet, keep the paper constantly pressed against the short side of the mirror. When done, touch it on the large side and give it to the person concerned.

1° If the person uses it as a talisman, he will take it with the right hand, make the sign of the cross and wear it like a scapular wrapped in a cloth. Its virtue lasts one year; at the end of this time, throw it in the fire.

2° If used it heal himself, he will also take it with his right hand, make the sign of the cross and attach it to his shirt so that it remains in contact with the skin where is the evil. Keep it for three or five days if you want to force it. At the end of this time, take (the patient or the operator) the packet, make the sign of the cross, put it in the fire, cover it with coal and leave immediately; when you set foot outside, say: "May God keep us."

The packet and the words serve multiple purposes. Note that the operator can make the packet at home, put it in his pocket and take it to the cursed person.

Care to take when returning from a
person you want to heal.

Going to a crossroads, the best is the
one that has four paths, but take the
first one you find. Throw some money
with force (a penny or other) in the middle of the crossroads, saying: "Here you
are, pick you up whoever can." And leave
without looking back.

To break a spell and see the
maleficient.

Buy a new earthen pot and its cover,
for five pennies of camphor, a packet
of needles, a heart of a Calf, at the least
you could use the heart of a female, all of
which without haggling. Securely lock the
door where you operate.

Place the heart on a clean plate and
insert the needles separately, repeating at
each of them the following words we are
well acquainted:

"Against such and such (if we knew the person or, when we will, we will pronounce his name), once *vassis atatlos vesul & cremus, verbo san hergo diboliâ herbonos,* twice *vassis atatlos, &c.,* thrice *vassis, &c.*"

Once the operation is complete, put the heart in the pot with the camphor and three drops of holy water; put the pot to heat on a fire at exactly 11 hours and a half, and let it boil there until an hour after midnight, at the very least. The next day bury the pot in the ground in an uncultivated place.

To see the maleficent, by boiling the pot, from the beginning to the end, and every five minutes approximately, repeat the words above while looking in the mirror, sometimes on one side, sometimes on the other. It is rare that one does not see his image pass here and there.

Nota. — Take great care not to go out, and that no one from the house goes out while the operation lasts. — It is good to give a packet (talisman) to the patient before beginning the operation.

It is necessary to make a novena, that is to say for nine other days at 11h30, either in the evening or in the morning, repeating the words above.

To lift a spell or deliver a house from Demons.

Give a packet (talisman) to the cursed person or hang it in the fireplace in a new cloth bag. If the person is insane, three masses must be said in three different parishes, while in the house, when the masses are being performed, the family must say together *The Apostle's Creed,* make the sign of the cross, say three *Pater* and three *Ave*, make the sign of the cross again and say the *Veni Creator.*

This done, place yourself to the South, having holy water in your left hand, blessed boxwood in your right, and say: "*O God of the South, O God of the East, O God of the West, O God of the North, corrupted evil spell that I should have on your lives.*"

Repeat these words three times and each time, take holy water and sprinkle it forcefully to the right and to the left. Make a novena by looking in the mirror, if you have one, with the aforementioned words.

To break and destroy a spell by means of the Black Rooster.

Take a black Rooster, place three drops of holy water in its beak and hang it by its legs in an attic where you will leave it for three complete days. When this time has elapsed, take it by the legs and bury it in the hot manure of a sheep's roof, taking care that no one can go and remove it. The maleficent will fall ill and die of languor in six months to a year.

By doing the operations above, pronounce the words that we have already made known: "Against such and such, once *vassis, &c.*" Take great care to lock the attic while the Rooster is there.

To chase away a person.

Take a Toad before sunrise or after sunset; (before or after the sun has set) stuff it camphor with a wooden or iron pin, even a nail; thread both jaws with the said pin, tie them with a wire and hang it in the chimney high enough so that it is not seen. By doing the above from beginning to end, say: "I blame you N., I want you to die, you who do so much harm. Against such and such, once *vassis, &c.*" Do a novena.

Same subject.

Take a sprig of wild Medlar, a sprig of Holly, and third of wild Hazel, each three feet long. Place them in a dry wood fire and burn them, beginning at one end. From the time they begin to burn until they are done, say as above and do the novena.

To divert a bad encounter.

Take three steps back, while continually looking at the person, and say: *"Against you, Verbo san Diboliâ herbonos."*

For nailing & make a person suffer.

Go to a cemetery, collect a nail from an old coffin, saying: "Nails, I take you so that you can help me to divert and hurt anyone I want; in the name of the Father, the Son and the Holy Spirit. Amen."

When you want to use it, trace Figure 10 on a piece of new board and drive the nail in the middle of the triangle while saying: *Pater noster*, until *in terra*. Then hit the nail with a stone, saying: "May you hurt N. until I pull you out of there."

Cover the area with a little dust and note it well; for you cannot cure the evil that it causes except by pulling the nail out while saying: "I remove you, so that the harm you have caused to N. ceases;

in the name of the Father, the Son and the Holy Spirit. Amen." Then pull out the nail and erase the characters, not with the same hand you made them, but with the other; because there would be danger for the maleficent.

To make a person suffer.

Perform on the last Friday of the month, in the morning, and having fasted. Take a fat piece of bacon, the size of an egg; prick it with pins (about thirty without counting them) while saying the known words: "Once *vassis atatlos, &c.*", place on it two branches of blessed twigs in the form of a cross and bury everything in an uncultivated ground.

THIRD PART

MARVELLOUS
SECRETS

The Castle of Belle.
To protect Horses and other domestic animals from all accidents and illness.

Take some salt on a plate; then having your back against the sunrise, and with the animals before you, pronounce the following, being on your knees, bareheaded:

"Salt which is made and formed at the Castle of Belle Saint Belle Elisabeth, in the name of Disolet, Solfée carrying salt, salt whose salt, I conjure you in the name of Gloria, of Doriante and Galianne her sister; salt I conjure you that you keep hold for me my lively horses of equine beasts who are present before God and before me, healthy and clean, drinking well, eating well, large and fat, that they may be at my will; salt whose salt, I conjure you by the power of glory, and by the virtue of glory, and in all my intention always of glory."

This being pronounced in the corner of the rising sun, go to the other corner following the course of this star, and there you will pronounce the above. You will do the same at the other corners. And when you are back where you started, repeat the same words again. Observe this throughout the ceremony to keep the animals in front of you at all times, because those who cross might be mad beasts.

Afterwards, circle your horses three times, sprinkling your salt on the animals, saying: "Salt, I throw you from the hand God has given me; Grapin, I take you, of you I await."

In the remainder of your salt, you will bleed the animal used to ride, saying: "Equine beast, I bleed you with the hand that God has given me; Grapin, I take you, of you I await."

It must be bled with a piece of hard wood, such as boxwood or pearwood.

Draw as much blood from whatever part you wish, whatever some capricious people may say, who attribute particular virtues to certain parts of the animal. We only recommend that when drawing blood, the animal's ass should be behind you. If it's a sheep, for example, you hold its head between your legs. Finally, after you've bled the animal, collect some of the horn from the right foot with a knife, divide it into two pieces and make a cross out of them; put this cross in a piece of new cloth, then cover it with your salt. Then take some wool, if you are working with sheep; otherwise take horsehair, and make a cross which you place in your cloth on the salt; you then place a second layer of salt on this wool or horsehair. You then make another cross of Paschal virgin wax or blessed candle; then you put the rest of your salt on top of it, and tie the whole thing into a ball with a string. With this ball, you will rub the animals as they leave the stable, if they are horses; if they are sheep, you rub them as they leave the sheepfold or the pen, pronouncing the words you used for the sprinkling of salt. Continue to rub them for one, two, three, seven, nine or eleven consecutive days. This depends on the strength and vitality of the animals.

Note that you should only do your sprinklings at the last word. When operating on horses, pronounce briskly; when it comes to sheep, the longer you take to pronounce, the better you will do. When you find horsehair in the collection of salt to be cast, you should only do them on salt and not elsewhere. All the guards begin on a Tuesday or a Friday at the crescent of the Moon; and in urgent cases, these observations are overridden. You must be careful not to let your bundles get damp, otherwise the animals would perish. They are usually carried in the gusset, but without burdening yourself with this useless care, do what expert practitioners do. Place them at home in some dry place, and worry not. We said above to take only the horn from the right foot to make the bundle.

Most people take horn from all four feet, and consequently make two crosses, since they have four pieces. This is superfluous and produces nothing more. If you do all the ceremonies of the four corners only at the corner of the rising sun, the herd will be less dispersed.

Observe that a wicked shepherd, who has a grudge against the one who replaces him, can cause him much grief, and even cause the flock to perish. Firstly, by means of the bundle, which he cuts into pieces and scatters, either on a table or elsewhere, or by a rosary novena, after which he wraps the bundle in it, then cuts the whole and scatters it, either by means of a mole or weasel, or by the pot or tare or cruet, finally by means of a frog or green treefrog, or a cod tail, which they put into an anthill, saying: "*Maudition, perdition, &c.*" (See the Enchiridion.)

They leave it there for nine days, after which they lift it out again with the same words, grinding it into powder and sowing it where the herd is to graze. They also use three pebbles taken from different cemeteries, and by means of certain words that we do not wish to reveal, they provoke emanations, cause scabies, and make as many animals die as they wish. We shall hereafter give the way to destroy these prestiges, by our ways of breaking guards and all curses.

Against glanders and colic in Horses.

Run your hand over the belly of the Horsey and say : "Horse (name the hair) belonging to N., if you have glanders, of whatever colour they may be, and abdominal cramps or colic, or of thirty-six kinds of other ailments, for whatever they may be, may God heal you as well as blessed Saint Eloy: in the name of the Father, and of the Son, and of the Holy Spirit." Then say five *Pater* and five *Ave* on your knees and make the Horse swallow a handful of gray salt dissolved in a pint of warm water.

So that the Lambs come back beautiful and strong.

T ake the first-born; failing that, the first to come to you. Lift it from the ground with its nose towards you, then say: "*Ecce lignum crucem in quo salus mundi crucem.*"

Put it back on the ground, lift it up again and say as above; do the same three times. When you have done this, you will pronounce with a low voice the orison of the day for the current day and that you will find in the Enchiridion.

To cure cancer or other ailment accessible to the eyes and fingers.

W ith the master finger (the longest) go around the ailment three times following the course of the sun, saying each time: "Evil pain (say its name) They say you have as many roots here as God has friends in heaven." Do this three days in a row before sunrise. When turning your finger, do not lift it off the skin. After each operation five *Pater* and five *Ave*.

Against the burn.

"Saint Lazarus and Our Lord Jesus Christ are going to a holy city. Saint Lazarus said to Our Lord: I hear a great noise up there. Our Lord said to him: It is a child who is burning, go ahead and you will heal him with your breath."

These words are said three times over the burns, each time breathing against them, then a compress well soaked in olive oil is applied. Five *Pater*, Five *Ave*.

To have stolen items returned.

Burn a good handful of Rue and another of *Savate* and say *The Apostle's Creed* three times, making the sign of the cross before and after.

To see at night in a vision, what you wish to know about the past or future.

In the evening before going to bed, re-produce Fig. 11 on virgin parchment. The two N.N. indicate where you must put your names as well as what you want to know. The free space between the two circles is intended to receive the name of the Angels you invoke. This done, recite the following orison three times and lie on your right side with your ear on the parchment.

Orison.

In the glorious name of the great living God, to whom, in all times, all things are present to him, I who am your servant N., Eternal Father, I beg you to send me your Angels who are written in this circle, and that they show me what I am curious to know and learn, by Our Saviour Jesus Christ. So be it.

When your orison is finished, lie down on your right side, and you will see in a dream what you desire.

To stop a Snake.

Throw after it, a piece of paper dipped in a solution of alum, and on which you have written with the blood of a kid goat: "Stop, fair one, here's a forfeit." Then whistle a wicker rod in front of it: if it is touched with this rod, it will die immediately, otherwise it will promptly flee.

To stop Horses and crew.

Trace on black paper in white ink the pentacle figured in Fig. 12 and throw this pentacle thus traced at the head of the horses, and say: "White or black horse, of whatever colour you may be, it is I who make you do it, I conjure you so you may not pull anymore with your feet as you do with your ears, nor can Beelzebuth break his chain."

For this experiment, you will need a nail forged during the midnight mass, which you will drive where the harness passes through. Failing that, take a scab and conjure it as follows:

"Scab, I conjure you in the name of Lucifer, Beelzebuth and Satanas, the three Princes of all devils, that you must stop."

During the three days before the day you wish to perform this operation, be careful not to do any Christian work.

Counter-Charm.
(for the previous)

"*Hostia sacra verra corrum*, while repelling the great devil of hell, all words, enchantments and characters that have been said, read and celebrated on the bodies of my lively horses, may they be broken and shattered behind me."

After this, repeat the orison which begins with these words: "Word, which has become flesh, &c." (See the Enchiridion.)

To seem to be accompanied by many.

Take a handful of sand, and conjure it thus: "Anachi, Jehova, Hælersa, Azarbel, rets caras sapor aye pora cacotamo lopidon ardagal margas poston eulia buget Kephar, Solzeth Karne phaca ghedolos salesetata."

Place the sand thus conjured into an ivory box with the powdered skin of a tiger snake. Then throw it into the air while reciting the conjuration and there will appear as many men as there are grains of sand; do this on the day and at the hour when the Sun is in the sign of Mary, the Virgin.

To make oneself invisible.

Take a black Cat, and a new pot, a mirror, a lighter, coal and tinder. Gather water from a fountain at the strike of midnight.

After you light your fire, and put the Cat in the pot. Hold the cover with your left hand without moving nor looking behind you, no matter what noises you may hear.

After having made it boil twenty-four hours, put the boiled Cat on a new dish. Take the meat and throw it over your left shoulder, saying these words: *"Accipe quod tibi do, et nihil ampliùs."*

Then put the bones one by one under the teeth on the left side, while looking at yourself in the mirror; and if they are do not work, throw them away, repeating the same words each time until you find the right bone; and as soon you cannot see yourself any more in the mirror, withdraw, moving backwards, while saying: *"Pater in manus tuas commendo Spiritum meum."*

Keep this bone out of sight of any profane. Afterwards, all you have to do is put it between your teeth to make yourself invisible.

Garters for travelling.

Leave your house on an empty stomach, walk to your left until you find a merchant selling ribbons. Buy a yard of white one; pay whatever is asked of you, and drop a liard in the shop, return home by the same route. The next day, do the same until you find a merchant selling feathers. Buy one cut, just as you bought the ribbon; and when you are back in your dwelling, write with your own blood on the ribbon, the characters of the Fig. 13 for the right garter, and the Fig. 14 for the left garter. When this is done, leave your house; on the third day, wear your ribbon and your quill; walk to your left until you find a pastry chef or a baker; buy a cake or a loaf of bread for two liards; go to the first tavern, order a half-bottle of wine, have the glass rinsed three times by the same person, break the cake or bread into three pieces; put the three pieces in the glass with the wine. Take the first piece and toss it under the table, without looking there, saying: "Irly, for you." Then take the second piece and toss it away, saying: "Terly, for you." Write on the other side of the garter the names of these two Spirits with your blood; toss away the third piece, saying: "Eirly, for you." Throw away the quill, drink the wine without eating, pay your due and leave. Being out of town, put on your garters; be careful not to mistakenly put the one that is for the right on the left, there is consequence. Stamp your foot three times on the ground, calling out the names of the Spirits: Irly, Terly, Erly, Balthazar, Melchior, Gaspard, let us walk. Then make your journey.

To walk without being tired.

Write on three silk ribbons, *Gaspard, Melchior, Balthazar*. Tie one of these ribbons above the right knee, without tightening it; the second above the left knee, and the third around the kidneys. Before setting out, swallow a small glass of anise in some broth or in a glass of white wine, and rub your feet with Rhue crushed in olive oil.

To prevent from eating at the table.

Nail under the table a needle that has been used to bury a dead man, and which had pierced his flesh, then say, "Coridal, Nardac, Degon." Then you will place a piece of Assa fœtida onto burning charcoal, and take your leave.

To win at games.

Gather the herb called *Morsus Diaboli* on the eve of St. Peter, before sunrise. Put it on the blessed stone for a day, then dry it, powder it and carry it with you. To pick it, you have to make this semicircle, with the names and crosses marked on Figure 15..

For game of dices.

"Dice, I conjure you in the name of Assizer and of Rassize, that they may come Raid and Grab in the names of Assia and Leugus." Note that you must wear the scapular made of clover leaves, as mentioned earlier.

To win at games.

During stormy weather, gather some four or five leaf clover, making over

them the sign of the cross, then say:
"Trifle or large Clover, I pick you in the
name of the Father, and of the Son, and
of the Holy Ghost, by the virginity of the
Holy Virgin, by the virginity of St John
the Baptist, by the virginity of St John the
Evangelist, that you may serve me in all
kinds of games." Then you have to say
five *Pater* and five *Ave*, and continue, "*El,
Agios, Ischyros, Athanatos.*" You will keep
this clover in a black silk bag that you will
wear like a scapular each time that you
play. At other times, take care to put it in
a safe place.

To win at lotteries.

B efore going to bed, you must recite
this orison three times. After which,
you will put it under the pillow, written
on parchment, on which a mass of the
Holy Spirit will have been said and, during
sleep, the Genie of your planet will come
to tell you the time when you must take
your ticket.

Orison.

Domine Jesu Christe, qui dixisti: Ego sum via, veritas et vita; ecce enim veirtatem dlexisti, incerta et occulta sapientæ tuae manifesta mihi adhuc quæ revelet in hâc nocte sicut itâ revelatum fuit parvulis solis, incognita et ventura anaque alia me doceas, ut possim omnia cognoscere, si et si sit; ita monstra milii mortem ornatam omni cibo bono, pulchrum et gratum pomarium, aut. quandam rem gratam; sin autem miuistra mihi ignem ardentem, vel aquam currentem vel uliam quamcunque rem quse Domino placeant et vel Angeli Ariel, Rubiel, et Barachiel sitis mihi multûm aniatores et factures ad opus istud obtinendum qnod cupio scire, videre, cognoscere et prævidere per illum Deum qui venturus est judicare vivos et mortuos, et sæculum per ignem. Amen.

You will say three *Pater* and three *Ave Maria*, for the souls in purgatory.

To be loved.

D raw some of your blood, on a spring Friday, put it in a small and new glazed earth pot with the testicles of a Hare and the liver of a Dove, and dry everything in an oven from which the bread is drawn. Reduce to a fine powder, which you will make swallow the person on whom you have intentions, approximately the quantity of half a drachma. And if the effect is not sufficient on the first occasion, increase up to three, and you will be loved.

To make a girl come to you, however modest she may be. Experiment of a marvellous power of the superior intelligences.

I t should be observed, from the first quarter to the waning of the moon, a very bright star between eleven and midnight; but before beginning do as follows.

Take a virgin parchment, on which you will write the name of the person whom you desire to come. The parchment must be cut in the manner shown on the first line of the following figure.

The two NN indicates the place for the names. On the other side of the parchment, write these words: MACHIDAEL BARESCHAS; then put the parchment on the earth, the names against the ground, your right foot on it and your left knee on the ground. Holding in the right hand a white wax candle that can last for an hour, look at the brightest star and say the following conjuration.

Conjuration.

I salute thee and conjure thee, O beautiful Moon and beautiful Star, as well as the bright light which I hold in my hand, by the air that is within me, and by the earth that I am touching. I conjure thee, by all the names of the Spirit princes that presides in you, by the ineffable name ON, which created everything, by you, beautiful Angel Gabriel with Prince Mercury, Michael and Melchidael. I conjure thee again, by all the Names of God, that you send to possess, torment, harass the body, the soul and the five senses of N., whose name is written on this parchment, so that she comes to me and fulfill my will, that she has no friendship for anyone in the world, especially for N. as long as she is indifferent towards me. May she cannot endure. May she be obsessed, suffer and tormented. Go, therefore, promptly Melchidael, Bareschas, Zazel, Tiriel, Malcha and all those who are under your command. I conjure thee, by the great living God, to send her speedily to satisfy my will. Me N., I promise to satisfy you.

Having repeated this conjuration three times, put the candle on the parchment and let it burn. The next day, take said parchment and put it in your left shoe. You leave it there until the person whom you have made this operation comes to find you.

It is necessary, in the conjuration, specify the day you want her to come and she will not be absent.

To make a girl dance nude.

On virgin parchment, write the characters of Figure 17 with the blood of a Bat, then place it on a blessed stone so that a Mass is said on it. After which, when you want to use it, place this occult character under the threshold of the door where the person you are thinking of must pass. As soon as she has passed by, you will see her burst into fury, taking off her clothes and stripping herself completely naked. If you do not remove the character, she will dance until she dies, making grimaces and contortions which will cause more pity than desire.

To prevent copulation.

For this experiment, you must have a new penknife, then, on a Saturday, at the precise time of Moon rise, while it is waning, you will trace with the point, behind the door of the room where the people sleep, the characters in Fig. 18, as well as the words, *Consummatum est*, and break the point of the penknife in the door.

To not be wounded by any weapon.

Recite three times in the morning when you get up and in the evening when retiring to bed: "I rise (or I go to bed) in the name of Jesus Christ who has been crucified for me. May Jesus bless me; may Jesus wants to lead me; may Jesus guard me; may Jesus desires to govern and lead me to eternal life, in the name of the Father, and of the Son, and of the Holy Ghost."

The following will be written on the sword or weapon you wish to use: Ibel, Ebel, Abel.

Against a sword strike.

Before going to fight, write on a ribbon of any colour the following two words: BUONI JACUM. Tighten your right wrist with this ribbon; fear not, defend yourself, and the sword of your enemy will never touch you.

For when going to an action (at war).

Say five *Pater* and five *Ave* in honour of the five wounds of Our Saviour. Then say three times, "I am going in the shirt of Notre-Dame; may I be enveloped by the wounds of my God, by the four crowns of heaven, by Mr. St John the Evangelist, St Luke, St Matthew and St Mark; may they guard me; may no man, woman nor lead, neither iron nor steel, wound me, cut me, nor crush my bones, for the peace of God." And when we have said the above, you have to swallow the following words written on white marrow: *Est principio, est in principio, est in verbum, Deum et tu phantu.* It is for twenty-four hours.

Against a firearm.

"Star who leads the weapon today, may I charm you *gige* I tell you, that you may obey me in the name of the Father and the Son and Satanis." Make a sign of the cross.

To Enchant Firearms.

Say: "God has a share in it and the devil has the exit," and when you fire, say the following while crossing your left leg over your right: *"Non tradas Dominum nostrum Jesum Christum. Maton. Amen."*

To make a weapon fail.

Take a new clay pipe, fitted with its brass cap, fill it with powdered Mandrake root, then blow through the pipe while silently pronouncing to yourself : "Abla, Got, Bata, Bata, Bleu."

FOURTH PART

THE HAND OF GLORY
THE BLACK HEN
THE GREAT EXORCISM

The Hand of Glory

Giving unlimited Gold and Silver.

Pull out the hair, with its root, from a mare in heat, closest to the nature, saying: "Dragne, Dragne." Secure the hair, and immediately buy a new earth pot with the cover, without haggling. Return home; fill this pot with water from a spring, up to two fingers near the edge. Place the said hair into the pot, which you must cover. Put it in a place where it cannot be seen by either you or others, because there would be danger.

After a period of nine days, and at the same time that you hid it, go uncover it; you will discover inside a small animal in the shape of a snake. He will stand upright; you will tell him immediately, "I accept the Pact." This done, you will take it without touching it with your hand; you will put it in a new box bought express-ly for the purpose without haggling: you will put wheat bran in it, nothing else; but you must not fail to give it to him every day; and when you want to have silver or gold, you will put in the box as much as you want to have, and you will lie down on your bed, putting your box near you, and sleep, if you want, for three or four hours. After this time, you will find double the money you put in; but you must be care-ful to put the same one back.

Note that the small figure, only comes by the force of the charm; so you cannot put more than 100 pounds at a time. But if, however, your planet gives you domin-ance over supernatural things, the serpent will be in the likeness of the second fig-ure of the same line as above; that is to say, he will have a face approaching the human face, and you will be able to put up to 1000 pounds; every day you will get twice as much. If you wanted to get rid of it, you can give it to whoever you want, provided that they accept it. Otherwise you will trace the signs and characters of Fig. 19 on virgin parchment which will be put in the box, and instead of the ordinary wheat bran, you will give to the little animal the bran from the flour on which a Priest will have said his first Mass, and it will die. Take care not to forget any circumstance; for there is no mockery in this affair.

The Black Hen.

Take a black Hen that has never laid eggs and which no Rooster has approached; take care when taking it not to make it scream. And for this you will go at 11 in the evening when it is sleeping to take it by the neck; you will only squeeze as much as necessary to prevent it from screaming. Go to a crossroads and at the stroke of midnight, make a circle with a cypress stick, stand in the middle and cut the body of the Hen in two while pronouncing these words three times: "*Eloïm, Essaïm, Frugativi, et appelavi.*"

Then turn facing towards the East, kneel and say an orison. This done, you will see the great appellation; then the foul Spirit will appear to you, in a scarlet laced garment, dressed in a yellow jacket and sea green breeches. His head, which will resemble that of a dog with donkey ears, will be surmounted by two horns, his legs and feet will be like those of a cow. He will ask for your orders, you will give them to him as you see fit, because he will no longer be able to refuse to obey you, and you will be able to make yourself the richest and therefore the happiest of all men.

THE GREAT EXORCISM

To dispossess either the human
creature, or unreasonable animals.

Demon, leave the body of N., by
the command of the God whom
I adore, and yield for the Holy Spirit. I
place the sign of the Holy Cross of Our
Lord Jesus Christ on your forehead. In the
name of the Father, and of the Son, and
of the Holy Spirit. I make the sign of the
Cross of Our Lord Jesus Christ over your
breast. In the name of the Father, and of
the Son, and of the Holy Spirit. Eternal
and Almighty God, Father of Our Lord
Jesus Christ, cast the eyes of your mercy
upon your servant N. whom you have
deigned to call to the right hand of faith,
heal his heart of all manner of elements

and misfortunes, and break all his chains
and bonds. Lord, open the door of your
glory by your goodness, so that, being
marked with the seal of your wisdom,
he may be free from the stench, attacks
and desires of the foul Spirit; and being
filled with the sweet odour of your boun-
ties and graces, he joyfully observes your
commandments in your Church; and ad-
vancing day by day in perfection, he is
made worthy of having received the salutary remedy for his faults, through your
holy Baptism, by the merits of the same
Jesus Christ Our Lord and God. Lord,
we beseech you to answer our prayers,
to preserve and protect what a charitable
love has made you redeem at the price
of your precious blood, and by the virtue of your Holy Cross, by which we are
marked. Jesus, protector of the poor and
afflicted, be favourable unto the people
you have adopted, making us partakers of
the New Testament, so that the letters of
promise may be fulfilled and received by
your grace what they can only hope for

through you, Jesus Christ Our Saviour,
who is our recourse, who made Heaven
and Earth. I exorcise you, creature, in the
name of God, the Father Almighty, and
by the love that Our Christ Jesus bears,
and by the virtue of the Holy Spirit; I
exorcise you by the great living God, who
is the true God that I adore, and by the
God who created you, who has preserved
all his chosen ones, who has commanded
his servants to bless him, for the benefit of those who believe in him, so that
everything becomes a salutary Sacrament
to drive out the enemy. It is for this rea-
son, Lord our God, that we beseech you
to sanctify this salt with your holy bene-
diction, and to make it a perfect remedy for those who receive it. May it remain in their bowels, so that they may be
incorruptible, in the name of Our Lord
Jesus Christ, who is to judge the Quick
and the Dead, and by the seal of the God
of Abraham, the God of Isaac, the God
of Jacob, the God who was appeared to
his servant Moses on Mount Sinai, who

drew the children of Israel out of Egypt,
giving them an Angel to protect them and
lead them day and night. I also beseech
you, Lord, to send your holy Angel to protect your servant N. and lead him to eternal life, in virtue of your holy Baptism. I
exorcise you, impure and rebellious Spirit,
in the name of God the Father, God the
Son, God the Holy Spirit; I command
you to leave the body of N., I adjure
you to withdraw in the name of the One
who gave Saint Peter his hand when he
was about to drown into the water. Obey
your God, cursed Demon, and obey the
sentence pronounced against you, and
honour the living God, honour the Holy
Spirit and Jesus Christ, sole-begotten Son
of the Father. Be gone, ancient serpent,
from the body of N. for the great God
commands you to do so; let your pride
be confounded and annihilated before
the sign of the Holy Cross, with which
we have been marked by the baptism and
grace of Jesus Christ. Consider that the
day of your torment approaches, and that

unbearable torments await you; that your judgment is irrevocable, that your sentence condemns you and all your companions to eternal flames, on account of your rebellion against your Creator. Therefore, accursed Demon, I command you to flee for the sake of God, whom I adore; flee by the Holy God, by the True God, by Him who said, and all was done: render honour to the Father, the Son and the Holy Spirit, and to the most holy and indivisible Trinity. I command you, unclean Spirit, whosoever you may be, to leave the body of this creature N. created by God, who is the same God, Our Saviour Jesus Christ, that today he may deign by his infinite bounty, to call you to the grace of partaking in his holy Sacraments which he has instituted for the salvation of all the faithful. In the name of God, who will judge the whole world by fire.

Behold the cross of Our Saviour Jesus Christ. † Flee, opposing parties, behold the lion of the tribe of Judah, root of David.

FIFTH PART

ORISONS

Thanksgiving.

God Almighty, heavenly Father, who created all things for the service and use- fulness of men, I return to you my very humble thanksgiving that, through your great goodness, you have allowed me, without risk, to be able to make a pact with one of your rebellious Spirits and to subjugate him to give me everything I might need.

I thank you, O Almighty God, for the bounty with which you filled me during this night; deign to grant me, frail creature, your precious favours. It is now, O great God! that I have known all the strength and power of your great promises, when you said to us: Seek, and you will find; knock, and it will be opened to you.

And as you have ordered and recom- mended us to relieve the poor, deign, O

great God, to inspire me with true feelings of charity, and allow me to spread on
such a holy work a large part of the goods
which the great Divinity has kindly willed
me to be fulfilled.

Do, O great God! that I may enjoy
with tranquillity these great riches of
which I am the possessor, and do not allow any rebellious Spirit to harm me in
the enjoyment of the precious treasures
of which you have just allowed me to be
the master.

Inspire me too, O great God! the
necessary feelings to be able to free myself from the claws of the Devil and all
evil Spirits. I place myself, great God the
Father, God the Son and the Holy Spirit,
under your holy protection.

Amen.

To guarantee from Evil Spirits.

O Almighty Father! O Mother, the most tender of mothers! O admirable example of the feelings and tenderness of mothers! O son, the flower of all sons! O form of all forms! Soul, Spirit, harmony and number of all things, preserve us, protect us, lead us, and be favourable to us.

Amen.

Pater.

Pater noster, qui es in caelis
sanctificetur nomen tuum
adveniat regnum tuum
fiat voluntas tua
sicut in caelo et in terra.
Panem nostrum quotidianum
da nobis hodie
et dimitte nobis debita nostra
sicut et nos dimittimus
debitoribus nostris
et ne nos inducas in tentationem
sed libera nos a malo.
Amen.

Ave.

Ave Maria, gratia plena
Dominus tecum
Benedicta tu in mulieribus ;
Et benedictus fructus ventris tui, Jesus !
Sancta Maria, Mater Dei,
Ora pro nobis, peccatoribus,
Nunc, et in ora mortis nostræ.
Amen.

Veni Creator.

Veni, creator, Spiritus,
Mentes tuorum visita,
Imple superna gratia
Quae tu creasti pectora.

Qui diceris Paraclitus,
Altissimi donum Dei.
Fons vivus, ignis, caritas
Et spiritalis unctio.

Tu septiformis munere,
Digitus paternae dexterae.
Tu rite promissum Patris,
Sermone ditans guttura.

Accende lumen sensibus
Infunde amorem cordibus,
Infirma nostri corporis
Virtute firmans perpeti.

Hostem repellas longius
Pacemque dones protinus;
Ductore sic te praevio
Vitemus omne noxium.

Per te sciamus da Patrem,
Noscamus atque Filium;
Teque utriusque Spiritum
Credamus omni tempore.

Deo Patri sit gloria,
Et Filio, qui a mortuis
Surrexit, ac Paraclito
In saeculorum saecula.
Amen.

The Apostle's Creed.

I believe in God, the Father Almighty, Creator of Heaven and earth;

And in Jesus Christ, His only Son Our Lord,

Who was conceived by the Holy Spirit, born of the Virgin Mary,

Suffered under Pontius Pilate, was crucified, died, and was buried.

He descended into Hell;

The third day He rose again from the dead; He ascended into Heaven,

And sitteth at the right hand of God, the Father Almighty;

From thence He shall come to judge the living and the dead.

I believe in the Holy Spirit,

The holy Catholic Church, the communion of saints,

The forgiveness of sins, the resurrection of the body,

And life everlasting.

Amen.

TABLE.

SECOND PART

CHARMS & COUNTER-CHARMS

THIRD PART

MARVELLOUS SECRETS

FOURTH PART

THE HAND OF GLORY, THE BLACK HEN, THE GREAT EXORCISM

FIFTH PART

ORISONS

THE BLACK DRAGON

Or the Infernal Forces
Subjugated to Man

Printed in Great Britain
by Amazon